Science
ACTIVITY BOOK

Penguin Random House

Editorial assistant Abigail Luscombe
Assistant editor Gunjan Mewati
Editor Sally Beets
Assistant art editor Aishwariya Chattoraj
Project art editor Jaileen Kaur
Illustrators Rachael Parfitt Hunt, Charlotte Milner
Jacket coordinator Issy Walsh
Jacket designer Clare Baggaley
DTP designer Sachin Gupta
Managing editors Jonathan Melmoth, Monica Saigal
Managing art editors Diane Peyton Jones, Romi Chakraborty
CTS manager Balwant Singh
Production manager Pankaj Sharma
Picture researcher Rituraj Singh
Pre-production producer Dragana Puvacic
Producer Basia Ossowska
Delhi team head Malavika Talukder
Creative directors Helen Senior, Clare Baggaley
Publishing manager Francesca Young
Publishing director Sarah Larter

First published in Great Britain in 2020
by Dorling Kindersley Limited
80 Strand, London WC2R 0RL

Copyright © 2020 Dorling Kindersley Limited
A Penguin Random House Company
10 9 8 7 6 5 4 3 2 1
001–316744–July/2020

Material in this publication was previously published in Look I'm a Scientist (2017)

A CIP catalogue record for this book is available from the British Library.
ISBN: 978-0-2414-1382-1

Printed and bound in China

A WORLD OF IDEAS:
SEE ALL THERE IS TO KNOW
www.dk.com

Q&A

You'll find the answers to all the activities at the back of the book!

Little minds have big ideas!

You don't need a **white coat** and a **fancy lab** to be a scientist. You already have everything you need to be the best scientist ever: **your brain** and **your amazing senses**!

Your science senses

Brain
Your brain is not one of your senses, but it gathers information from them all and tries to understand it.

Hearing
There are so many noises to listen to! What can you hear?

Sight
Super scientists use their eyes for looking really, really carefully. Scientists wear goggles to protect their eyes.

Smell
Use your nose to find smelly clues!

Taste
Your tongue is great at tasting different flavours.

Touch
Your skin tells you how things feel. Be careful with objects that might be hot, cold, sharp, or that might hurt.

Let's see what we can do!

Curious questions

Science is about asking questions, as much as answering them. Here are some questions to ask yourself as you play.

- What will happen if I do this?

- What can I hear, smell, see, taste, and feel?

- Why did that happen?

- Does the same thing always happen?

- How can I find out more?

Ooey gooey slime

Mix up your own easy-peasy **slime**. Then see how it acts as both a **liquid** and a **solid**.

You will need:

spoon
bowl

2 cups
cornflour

+

1 to 2 cups
washing-up liquid

+

food
colouring

+

1 to 2 cups
warm water

1 In a bowl, **mix** the cornflour, washing-up liquid, and a few drops of food colouring.

2 Add **water** and mix until your slime is **runny** but **thick**.

pour

mix

Let it flow

Hold the slime in your hands and watch it **flow** through your fingers like a **liquid**.

SENSE-ible science

Can you feel the slime change as you play?

How does the slime smell? Do you like it?

Is the slime squelching in the bowl?

Do you think your slime is a liquid or a solid?

squash and squeeze

Roll it

If you **roll up** the slime, the tiny bits of cornflour inside squash together and the slime becomes **hard** like a **solid**.

Can you think of other liquids and solids?

Liquids

Liquids flow and can change the shape that they take.

water

juice

Solids

Solids are stiff and hold their shape.

spoon

brick

Place a sticker here when you're done.

Iceberg animal rescue

Water is a **liquid**, but what happens when it gets very cold? It freezes into **ice** – a **solid**! Make an **iceberg**, then **melt the ice** to rescue the animals.

You will need:

water

+

blue food colouring

+

plastic tub

+

toy animals

+

salt

+

sponge

1
Pour **water** and a few drops of food colouring into a freezable tub. Add your **animals**.

It's getting a bit crowded!

2
Put the tub and your toy animals in the **freezer** overnight.

Adult ALERT!

3
Is the iceberg frozen? Turn the tub **upside down** until your iceberg pops out.

6

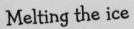

To the rescue!

Melting the ice

Scatter some salt on the iceberg to see what happens! Does it **melt** the ice?

> I'm free!

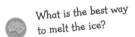
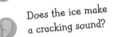

SENSE-ible science

- What is the best way to melt the ice?
- Does the ice make a cracking sound?
- Can you see the ice melting back to liquid water?
- Can you feel the difference between the ice and water?

Squeeze

Pour **warm** water on the ice, or squeeze it on with a sponge.

From ice to water

If water gets cold enough, the molecules (the tiny water bits) stop moving. The water goes stiff and turns to ice (it freezes from a liquid to a solid). Melting is the opposite of freezing.

solid ice

liquid water

Place a sticker here when you're done.

Blowing in the wind

Air is all around you. When air moves from one place to another, we call it **wind**. You can't see air, but it can be **strong** enough to blow your hat off!

Adult ALERT!

Attaching the screw eyes can be tricky. Ask an adult for help.

Hear the wind

You can make simple **wind chimes** with sticks. Hang them outside then listen to the wind **bang** the sticks together.

You breathe in and breathe out air with your lungs. You can use this air to blow on a paper windmill and make it spin.

string

screw eye

stick

paint to decorate

Complete the picture

Windmills use **wind** to make **energy**. Use a pen or pencil to draw the other half of this windmill – remember, it's **symmetrical**!

embroidery hoop or coat hanger

ribbons

SENSE-ible science

How does the wind feel in your hair?

Does the wind smell of anything? Why?

Can you think of ways that wind is useful?

See the wind

Make this rainbow **wind catcher** then watch the wind move the ribbons. Thread ribbons onto a hoop and hold it up outside. The wind will **lift the ribbons** like a kite. Can you see which way the wind is blowing?

Place a sticker here when you're done.

Brilliant balloons

Balloons are great to **play** with and for **experiments**. Take **a big breath in** and blow into your balloon to fill it with **air**. Then try these tricks.

Hair-raising electricity

Rub the balloon on your hair. Then lift the balloon above your **head**. What happens to your **hair**?

Rubbing the balloon on your hair makes a special kind of energy called **static electricity**. This makes your hair stick to the balloon.

It's electric!

I'm powered by electricity.

Balloon **rocket**

Thread the string through a paper drinking straw.

tape

balloon

Tie up the string tightly.

Thread string through a straw and tie it up tightly at both ends. Blow up your balloon, pinching the end closed. Tape it to the straw. **Ready, steady... Let go!**

When you let go, air rushes out of the balloon and pushes it forwards. How fast will it go?

Make a hovercraft

Stick a pop-up bottle cap onto an old CD or DVD. Pull a blown-up balloon on top. Then open the cap. **Push your hovercraft and watch it glide** along the table!

Air flows out of the balloon and through the cap. This makes an air cushion under the disc and lifts the hovercraft a tiny bit off the table.

Place a sticker here when you're done.

Tiny bubbles

You can make **great bubbles** by trapping **air** inside **soapy water**. These bubbles are small and super soft.

You will need:

soap

cheese grater

+

warm water

plastic tub

+

hand mixer

food colouring

Play with your bubbles, but DON'T EAT THEM!

1

Very carefully, **grate the soap** into little bits. Be careful of your fingers!

Adult ALERT!

2

Add the grated soap to warm water and mix it around until it **dissolves**.

3

Whizz up bubbles in your mixture with a hand mixer until they make a thick foam that holds its shape.

soft and squishy

Adult ALERT!

4

Add food colouring to make your bubbles **more colourful**.

What **shapes** can you **make?**

What shape is a bubble?

Place a sticker here when you're done.

13

BIG bubbles

Use a hula hoop to make these **HUGE** bubbles!
How tall can you make them?

You will need:

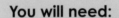

paddling pool
half-full of water

+

1 bottle
washing-up
liquid

hula
hoop

+

1 bottle
glycerine
(optional)

Glycerine only
works if you
make your
bubble mix a few
days ahead.

Glycerine makes
bubbles stronger.

How **big** is your **bubble?**

Word scramble

Can you help unscramble these bubble-related words?

MOAF _ _ _ _

OASP _ _ _ _

URSBT _ _ _ _ _

EBLBUB _ _ _ _ _ _

Mix all your ingredients in a **paddling pool**. Dip a **hula hoop** into the mix and **slowly lift it** out to make a long bubble.

Wow! This bubble is taller than me!

hula hoop

SENSE-ible science

 Can you see colours in your big bubbles?

 Do the big bubbles feel the same as the tiny bubbles?

 What other objects could you use as a bubble wand?

Place a sticker here when you're done.

Hear that sound?

When objects **touch** each other, they **vibrate** (move side to side). Your ears pick up the **vibrations** in the air and your brain turns them into **sounds.**

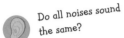
Musical bottles

Fill glass bottles with water. When you **tap** the bottles, the water and the air inside them **vibrate**. Depending on how much water and air they contain, the bottles make **different sounds.**

wooden spoon

tap tap

16

Be a tabletop scientist

There's lots of **easy-peasy science** you can do while you're waiting for your dinner. These two tabletop experiments play with **light** to **trick your eyes**.

> Your drawing has to be facing either left or right, but not straight on.

Mirror spoon

Look at your reflection in a **shiny spoon**. Then turn the spoon over. The **curve** of the spoon changes your reflection! Which side makes your face turn **upside-down**?

The ladybird trick

Draw a picture on a piece of paper and hold it **behind a glass of water**. Slowly move the glass towards you. Look through the glass to see the ladybird **turn around**.

What can you see inside the spoon?

Which way is the ladybird facing?

Place a sticker here when you're done.

Let's make a **potion**

Be a **science wizard** with this awesome potion experiment. This is a real **chemical reaction** you can do at home. It's messy, so be prepared!

You will need:

vinegar + washing-up liquid

+

jar

+

food colouring + biodegradable glitter

+

spoon + baking soda

1

Don't forget your goggles!

Half fill a glass jar with **vinegar** and squeeze in a little **washing-up liquid**.

Make *your potion* magical!

2

Add a few drops of food colouring and some glitter. Give the mixture a **good stir**.

3

Add a big spoonful of **baking soda** and **stir** it in. Quickly take out the spoon and **watch what happens**.

Fizzy chemistry

When vinegar and baking soda meet, they **react**. They make a gas called carbon dioxide. This gas makes lots of bubbles.

SENSE-ible science

 Does your potion make a noise?

 Can you describe how your potion smells?

 What do the bubbles feel like?

FIZZ!

Place a sticker here when you're done.

The Milky Way

Make these amazing milky **planets** and watch the colours **swirl** round and round as the **milk** tries to escape from the **washing-up liquid**.

You will need:

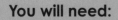

whole milk + food colouring

glass dish

+

washing-up liquid

+

biodegradable cotton buds

Real planets have swirls too. These are usually huge storm clouds.

1 Pour **milk** into a dish or jar lid and add a few drops of **food colouring**.

2 Dip a cotton bud in **washing-up liquid**. Swirl the cotton bud around in the milk and watch what happens.

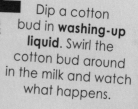

SENSE-ible science

- What happens when the colours mix?
- Do you know the names of any planets?
- Do your milky planets look like real planets?

Our galaxy

At night, our galaxy looks like a white starry path, so we call it the **Milky Way**.

Swirling milk

The washing-up liquid makes the **fat** inside the milk move around in all directions. By adding colour, you can see the milk **swirl and twirl**.

Place a sticker here when you're done.

Homemade playdough

Playdough is even **better** when you make it yourself! **Mix** your ingredients together to make a really squishable dough.

You will need:

 +

2 cups plain flour   1 cup salt

+

2 tablespoons oil

 +

2 cups water   2 teaspoons cream of tartar

+

pan   spoon

+

food colouring (optional)

1

Pour **all the ingredients** (except the food colouring) into a saucepan.

water

cream of tartar

salt

oil

flour

2

Adult ALERT!

Place the pan on a **medium heat**. Mix everything together until the ingredient form a **dough**.

3

Let your dough cool, then add food colouring. Now **squeeze** the dough until it's **smooth and soft**.

Play with your playdough

Your printing tool kit:

rolling pin

leaves, pine cones, and flowers

cutters

SENSE-IBLE SCIENCE

What objects can you print in your playdough?

Does your playdough smell of anything?

What prints can you see most clearly?

Can you describe how your playdough feels?

Prints and shapes

Roll your playdough flat with a rolling pin. Then use objects to make **really bumpy prints** or cut out **fun shapes**.

Place a sticker here when you're done.

23

Let it snow!

Snowflakes are made when **tiny ice crystals** inside clouds stick together. You can make **pretend snow**, then build your very own **snowpeople**!

You will need:

2 cups
baking soda

bowl

2 cups
shaving foam

1

Mix the ingredients with your hands. Your snow should be **crumbly** but **stick together** if you pat it together into a **snowball**.

Mix it!

Can you make a **snowball?**

2

If the mixture is **too crumbly**, add more shaving foam. If it's **too wet**, add more baking soda.

Word search

It is getting chilly outside. Can you find all of these snowy words?

Snowman ☒
Ice ☐
Snow ☐
White ☐

Cold ☐
Frozen ☐
Chill ☐

F	A	W	H	I	T	E
S	N	O	W	M	A	N
E	C	I	D	E	J	W
C	H	I	L	L	S	O
R	F	R	O	Z	E	N
B	U	S	C	D	M	S

SENSE-ible science

 Does your snow feel like real snow?

 Can you hear your snow squelching?

 Have you ever seen real snow?

3

Roll two snowballs to make your snowperson's **body** and **head**. Try adding googly eyes to decorate it.

Now use the stickers to give me a face, then we can all chill out together!

Place a sticker here when you're done.

25

When tiny things get big

Magnifying glasses help scientists look at things **very**, **very** closely. Try it! You might **see** things you'd **never noticed** before.

How does it work?

When you get closer to things, you can see them in **more detail**. But if you look at something too closely, it will look **blurry**. A magnifying glass has a **curved lens** that makes things look **closer**, without making them blurry.

Try it yourself! Grab a magnifying glass and look at things on this page and around you. It's your turn to be a scientific observer.

Woodland count

There's lots to look at in this busy nature scene. Write down how many of these things you can find.

1.   2.   3.   4.   5.

Play with clouds

Clouds can be **fluffy**, **puffy**, or **wispy**, but they all have one thing in common – they are made of water.

Are you painting me?

Cloud painting

Place a mirror on the ground outside. Can you see the **clouds** in the mirror? Use a paintbrush and shaving foam to **colour** them in.

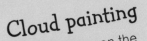
paintbrush

mirror

shaving foam

Dot-to-dot

Join the numbers from 1 to 45 to reveal what animal the cloud looks like.

Cloud spotting

When you're out and about, look up at the **sky**. What **shapes** can you spot in the clouds?

What are rainbows?

When sunlight shines through raindrops, the raindrops split the light into lots of colours. This makes a rainbow.

Clouds are made up of tiny droplets of water. When the droplets fall, they become rain. What do you think clouds would feel like to touch?

Place a sticker here when you're done.

Look, you're a scientist!

To prove a **new discovery**, most scientists follow the same set of **rules**. You can follow it too. Think about the experiments you have done. Can you follow **the scientific method**?

1. What is this?

When scientists observe something interesting, they come up with a theory about it to find out more. **Scientists call this theory a "hypothesis".**

2. What will happen?

Before trying out their hypothesis, scientists try to guess what the answer will be. **Scientists call this a "prediction".**

3. Time to play

Scientists love to play to try out their ideas. They have a go. Sometimes it goes wrong and they try to fix it. **Scientists call this an "experiment".**

A scientist's work is never done. There's always more to ask, more to discover, and more fun to be had!

4. What does it all mean?

Scientists think about what happened in their experiment and what they can learn from it. **Did you predict what would happen? Was it a surprise?**

Well done! You are a scientist!

Answers

Pages 14–15 Word scramble: FOAM; SOAP; BURST; BUBBLE.
Pages 26–27 Woodland count: 1. six; 2. two; 3. one; 4. five; 5. two.

Pages 8–9 Complete the picture:

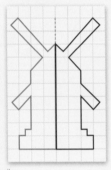

Pages 24–25 Word search:

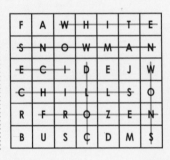

Pages 28–29 Dot-to-dot:

ACKNOWLEDGEMENTS

Dorling Kindersley would like to thank Katie Lawrence
for proofreading this book.

The publisher would like to thank the following for
their kind permission to reproduce their photographs:
(Key: a-above; b-below/bottom; c-centre; f-far; l-left; r-right; t-top)

9 Dreamstime.com: Digikhmer (tl). **iStockphoto.com:** borchee (Sky).
27 Dorling Kindersley: Natural History Museum, London (r/background).
28–29 Getty Images: Navaswan/The Image Bank (t/Clouds).
29 Getty Images: Darren Pearson (dariustwin)/Moment Select (tr).

All other images © Dorling Kindersley
For further information see: www.dkimages.com